Selling to State and Local Government

Understanding the Government Buyer

By

Charles A. Harris

1663 Liberty Drive, Suite 200
Bloomington, Indiana 47403
(800) 839-8640
www.authorhouse.com

This book is a work of non-fiction. Names of people and places have been changed to protect their privacy.

First published by AuthorHouse 09/27/04

ISBN: 1-4184-6073-7 (e)
ISBN: 1-4184-6072-9 (sc)

Printed in the United States of America
Bloomington, Indiana

This book is printed on acid-free paper.

INTRODUCTION

For some reason you bought this book, borrowed this book, or are looking at it in a bookstore. So you must have some sort of interest in selling to state and local government. Perhaps you are an experienced sales professional thinking about expanding into the public sector. Maybe you are an experienced public sector sales pro looking for a couple of tips. You may be a person completely new to sales and considering the public sector as your starting point. Or you may possibly be a government purchasing officer trying to keep a step ahead of us sales pros! So lets start off by making sure you have the correct book for you.

Is This Book For You?

This book is for new or experienced sales professionals interested in entering the rewarding world of selling to state and local government. It is for sales pros with little or no government selling experience who are trying to decide if a move to public sector sales is the right one. It is not intended for the sales professional with many years of government sales experience. The seasoned government sales pro will already know most of what is in this book, as well as an awful lot that is not!

What is the Purpose of This Book?

This book is a brief introduction to the world of state and local government selling. Its purpose is to give the new or experienced sales professional a high level overview of government selling. It will give you a general "lay of the land" so to speak. After reading this book you should have a clear idea if public sector sales is for you. And if you decide it is, you should have a good idea what it is about and what to expect.

This IS NOT a book about how to sell. If you are new to sales, this will be a useful book with regard to assisting you with the selection of your target customer. But you will need a firm grounding in basic sales skills. For this I would recommend Ziglar on Selling by Zig Ziglar, and AMA Handbook for Successful Selling by Bob Kimball.

So if you are still with me, read on and enjoy. Selling to state and local government is not for everyone. But the rewards can be great for those who accept the challenge!

TABLE OF CONTENTS

CHAPTER I

What is State and Local Government?

First of all, why do we choose to discuss state and local government separate from the Federal government? Well, as a sales professional the process of selling to the Federal government is very different from selling to other public sector entities. The Feds have their own set of procurement rules and regulations that defy and surpass the burdensome regulations of local government procurement. It is an entirely different market. So this book will deal strictly with state and local government.

So what exactly is "State and Local Government"? The simple answer is any government entity that does not fall under the Federal government. State government is pretty easy to define. It is any State and it's departments, instrumentalities, agencies, and other entities authorized under the state's constitution. Pretty simple. But what about local government? Well that is a much broader term. The obvious members of this group are cities and counties. But local governments cover a much broader base than that. In addition to the county and municipal governments (cities, towns, boroughs, villages, etc.), there are many entities that may not be quite as visible. These include:

- school districts
- port authorities
- transportation authorities
- bridge authorities
- water and sewer districts
- turnpike authorities
- university systems
- public health systems

As you can see, state and local government covers a very wide piece of the selling landscape.

CHAPTER II

Why Sell to State and Local Government?

I once lived in the Midwest working for a large international technology company. I was a pre-sales consultant with the public sector group. Some companies call this position sales consultant, sales engineer, marketing consultant, or solution consultant. I worked closely with the sales rep in all accounts. As a pre-sales guy my responsibilities involved responding to the functional and technical requirements of RFPs, preparing custom solutions, and conducting product demonstrations to customers. My hope was to work my way into a direct sales position. Eventually I was offered a direct sales territory based out of the

New York area. It was a very exciting time. The company paid for the entire move including all household goods, cars, and trips back to the Midwest to sell our old home. They moved the family and put us up in a corporate housing apartment while we were house hunting. The job seemed to be going great. In fact, I closed my first account while we were still in temporary housing! We moved into a house, moved our furniture in, enrolled our daughter in school, and finally started to feel settled. Then one Wednesday morning on our weekly conference call (about three months after our relocation) the announcement was made that the business unit was being dissolved at the end of the month. We had about 30 days to find another job. As you can imagine the moment the call ended every cell phone and email was buzzing. I am quite sure the employment websites had more than their share of hits that afternoon. Throughout the course of the next few weeks, some of us were offered positions in various business units of the company while others were encouraged to "explore other opportunities". I was fortunate enough to be offered a choice of two positions.

One was a desirable position selling to manufacturing companies. The other was a position selling to state and local government agencies. As you can guess by the title of this book, I chose to take the position selling to the public sector clients. Many people I knew reacted as you might expect: "Are you nuts? Those sales cycles take forever!" "What are you, some kind of masochist?" So why did I want to sell to the public sector? Or more importantly, why do you want to sell to the public sector?

According to the U.S. Census Bureau, in 1996 the total direct expenditure for state and local governments in the United States was $1,247,435,978,000! Yes, you counted the correct number of commas. That is over $1.2 Trillion. Do you need another reason?

So why would you want to sell to the public sector? Simple, to make money! Depending on what you sell and how your company sells it, signing and keeping government clients and customers can be a very lucrative business! It is sometimes a war of attrition, but for those with patience and persistence, there can be less serious competition. Many companies have some idea that there is money to be made selling to public sector. They assign an unsuspecting sales rep to pursue government accounts without the slightest idea what they are doing. Usually after several months of frustration and being thrown out of deals for failure to comply with purchasing rules or procedures, they blame the rep and decide that public sector business is not very profitable. At this point they stop actively targeting public sector opportunities. But every now and then an RFP (Request for Proposal) hits the street that is too lucrative to ignore, so they jump on it. This scenario is all too common. What it means for those of us willing to invest the time and energy required to become public sector experts, is that in any particular deal we only face a handful of serious competitors. The rest are pretenders!

CHAPTER III

Is State and Local Government Right for You?

Several years ago I left sales and began working in state government. At one point I was part of a selection team reviewing HR/payroll computer software systems for the entire state. We observed several presentations over a several week period. But one of the software presentations really stands out in my memory. For those of you in the software industry this setting will sound all too familiar. We were in a large conference room with a projector screen in front. There were about forty of us in the room (representatives from several different agencies). The presenter had a computer connected to a projector and she demonstrated the software for the group.

Many people in the audience were less than receptive to the idea of computerizing something they had been doing manually "just fine for the last thirty years". Some of the group were certified Luddites. The presenter was a very attractive young lady. She was dressed professionally and was well rehearsed. She had a clear speaking voice and her delivery was smooth. She knew her product well. The only problem she had was her audience. Most of us are familiar with the old saying "there is no such thing as a stupid question". Well, I must tell you that there are indeed stupid questions. There were a few folks in the room who had decided well in advance that no system would ever be able to do the job right. So they scoffed, complained, and cross-examined the poor woman. Throughout the day they threw a ridiculous array of "what-if" questions at her. "What if such and such happened and we had to do such and such?" the scenarios being presented were unbelievably absurd "what if we have a flood and the computer data is destroyed and there is a tornado at the first backup site in Texas and an earthquake destroys the secondary backup site in California"?

After a few hours, this heckling was obviously wearing her down. Finally the group became fixated on some miniscule oddity with regard to the way some process was performed at the state. I cannot remember what it was. All I remember is that it was a quirky little thing the state did, it did not make any sense whatsoever to do it that way, and it was a very simple process to change to a more standard way of doing things. But this odd little process was so far outside the standard way of running a payroll, that the computer system being demonstrated could not accommodate it. After being badgered about this perceived shortcoming the presenter had finally had enough. She let loose. "Of course our system cannot do it that way." "Why would you want to keep doing it that way?" "We have hundreds of clients in corporate America and I can tell you right now nobody out in the *real world* does it that way!" She was the right person in the wrong market.

Government selling can be tough. No, let me rephrase that. Government selling IS tough. It takes a special kind of person. There are negatives and positives in selling to the public sector. This is covered in more detail in the following chapters. I will be brief here but I won't mince words. The sales cycles can be very long. The processes can be Byzantine. The prospects can drive you completely crazy with their seeming inability to make decisions. Handling a sales cycle and covering all the requirements with the large number of people involved can seem like trying to clean up a hundred gallons of jelly with a lawn rake. Breaking into a public sector organization that has no experience buying from your company can take a lot of time and resources. However, once you become a trusted and reliable vendor, they will have a tendency to stick with you (provided you continue to offer excellent service and keep your prices competitive). A product or service being used in one department can often expand into an organization-wide adoption. You have the potential to take small deals and grow them over time. Public sector selling is a long-term proposition. I repeat:

Public Sector Selling is a Long Term Proposition!

This can be good or bad for you depending on your situation. First of all, you must assess if selling to the public sector is right for you and for your circumstance. There are several factors that influence how successful you will be selling to the public sector. The two main areas to evaluate are:

#1 – Your company (product, marketing, contracts, RFP support, and comp plan)

#2 – Yourself (family situation, selling style)

Lets look at some of these factors starting with your company.

Your Company's Product or Service

It is extremely important that your product or service has a practical application in the particular area of Public Sector you are trying to sell to. Fortunately the public sector market is broad enough that you can generally find a fit somewhere. For most products, it does not matter what organization you are selling to. An example could be someone working for a paper product firm selling paper towels and toilet tissue. Some things are done exactly the same way in the public sector as they are in the private sector! But suppose you work for a risk management firm trying to sell consulting and actuarial services to a government employee pension fund? You had better be selling consultants, actuaries, and a methodology with a track record in public sector. You cannot force a square peg into a round hole here. There are to many competitors with round pegs. Many firms have sales pros and often business units 100% dedicated to the public sector. Some firms actually sell only to the public sector. This does not mean you need a separate public sector division in your company to compete. But it does mean that your product or service must have a good public sector fit out of the box.

Your Company's Marketing

This is one of my pet peeves but I will try not to digress too far. I cannot believe the amount of marketing dollars wasted on sales collateral and advertisements ostensibly aimed at the public sector but with no public sector message. Many companies take their generic marketing material, put a picture of a capital building or something of the sort, and change the title to read "XYZ Solutions for Government". But as the prospect reads through the brochure or magazine ad, they see phrases such as "drive sales revenue", "create customer loyalty" and "drive shareholder value". The public sector buyers understand two things when they see this type of marketing material:

#1 – You do not know anything about public sector.

#2 – You are too lazy to even pretend you know something about it!

The other mistake often made in marketing is with regard to customer success stories or reference lists. Your company may be extremely proud that "88 of the top 100 manufacturers have used our performance management consulting services to cut costs". But that means absolutely nothing to a city HR director. Not only does it fail to help your cause, it most likely has a negative impact. She knows that cutting costs in the manufacturing sector by way of performance management most likely involves workforce reduction. So not only are you clueless as to how the public sector operates, you are most likely going to recommend something that will be political suicide for anyone attempting to implement your recommendation. Which will also mean the person who selected you as the vendor and granted you the contract will have severely limited their future career options! Companies with this type of marketing material often respond to RFPs, never make the short list, and then wonder what happened!

Now please keep in mind that generic marketing material is fine for generic commodity products. As in the paper supply example, there is nothing wrong with "our paper towels are strong, absorbent, and the highest quality available for the price". The same is true with regard to references. Providing restroom supplies for a manufacturing facility with 2,000 employees is not much different than providing restroom supplies to a government facility with 2,000 employees.

Your Company's RFP Support

We will discuss RFPs in more detail later. The RFP is the formal Request For Proposal that is often required by law for government entities making procurements over a specific dollar threshold. It is much more than a document. It is an entire process. Your company must have both the resources and the patience to properly respond to RFPs. Responding to an RFP is not rocket science, but it requires a great deal of attention to detail. But most importantly, it requires that your company be able to follow the process and meet the requirements. If your company cannot respond properly to RFPs, you will have serious difficulty selling to the public sector.

Of course there are also many products can be purchased by way of a blanket government schedule that does not require an RFP process. But most large competitive procurements require the process.

Your Company's Contract Policies

Negotiating contracts with government entities can be perhaps one of the most frustrating and challenging parts of the entire government sales process. Your company has to be able to meet government contract requirements. If your company has not engaged in much government work before, your legal team has some work ahead of them. Government contracts often contain terms that that send most legal eagles running for the door. What makes this particularly tough for you (the sales pro) is that by the time you get to the contracts, you have already prospected, made contact, discovered a need, fit your product to the need, responded to an RFP, given product presentations, managed to get selected over the other competitors, and in essence have already "made the sale". But just as you are ready to get some ink on paper and collect that big commission check, your counsel says "there is no way we can ever agree to this". Then the customer's counsel looks at your requirements and says, "The statutes won't allow us to do this".

Hopefully your company has experience with government contracts. If not, you should obtain copies of other contracts executed with the particular government entity you want to sell to (fortunately with government organizations, this is generally public information). Get these in front of your legal team to get their feedback. Even though your company may not currently sell to government, you may have a lawyer on staff that has public sector experience from a previous position.

Your Company's Comp Plan

The manner in which you are compensated has a huge impact on your ability to succeed in public sector sales. As we discussed earlier, public sector sales is a long-term proposition. It is a long sales cycle and it usually involves some heavy-duty price concessions. However, you also generally have a long-term client and a lot of long-term opportunity for up selling and add on selling. Some comp plans make this a very lucrative environment. Others make this a recipe for failure.

Let's use an automotive fleet dealer as an example. This company sells cars and light trucks. The vehicles are modified to suit the needs of government organizations. For example cars may be outfitted with special equipment so they can be utilized as police cars and trucks can be equipped with road repair or snow removal equipment. Sales pros are paid 6% on vehicle sales. For the sake of keeping the example simple we will assume that every account you sell in this market space is identical. Let's say your typical account takes almost a year of work to complete the initial sales cycle. Then the customer buys 50 cars at $10,000 each to replace some motor pool cars that are being retired. The customer is happy with your company and every year after that buys another 50 cars. In year 3 the customer also decides to buy 25 trucks at $20,000 each and continues to buy 25 more each year after that. Lets see what happens in three scenarios:

Scenario #1

Your company is divided into new account reps and existing account reps. You are paid on vehicle sales only. You are paid only on new accounts. Once the account becomes an active customer, it is turned over to an existing account rep. You worked this account for most of the year and you were paid $30,000 in commissions (6% X $500,000). The account is then turned over to the existing account rep. Every year after that HE collects $30,000 on each new car order and in year three collects $30,000 on the truck order. And all he did was have lunch with the client four or five times during the year and get the contract signed! So your revenue stream for this account looks like this:

Year 1 - $30,000

Year 2 - $0

Year 3 - $0

Year 4 - $0

Year 5 - $0

Year 6 - $0

If your comp plan is setup this way, public sector may not be for you. If you close one new account a year, you are working hard for not much in the way of commissions. Hopefully you have a very generous base salary and a small quota!

Scenario #2

Your company does not have dedicated existing customer reps and allows you to keep any account you sell and you get credit for any future sales. However you are credited for car sales only. If your account is interested in trucks, a different rep is brought in. So when you close the deal, you will get your $30,000. But you also will also earn $30,000 every year after that as long as they keep replacing 50 cars a year with your product. Public sector is now starting to look pretty good. Remember that it is a long-term proposition. Your revenue stream for this account looks like this:

Year 1 - $30,000

Year 2 - $30,000

Year 3 - $30,000

Year 4 - $30,000

Year 5 - $30,000

Year 6 - $30,000

If you close one new account a year, the reorder commissions will start to add up to quite an annuity.

Scenario #3

The same as scenario #2, only you have no product restriction. If you sell a new account you get to keep it. Everything they buy going forward from your company is through you. So when you close the deal, you will get your $30,000. You also will earn $30,000 every year after that for the car reorder. But in year three you will also earn $30,000 (6% X $500,000) for the truck sale. Now your sales stream for this one account looks like this:

Year 1 - $30,000

Year 2 - $30,000

Year 3 - $60,000

Year 4 - $60,000

Year 5 - $60,000

Year 6 - $60,000

If you sell one new account every year, these commissions start to overlap and you will be earning more than you know what to do with! Looking at these from a different perspective assuming one new account a year your total commission stream in each scenario looks like this:

SCENARIO #1

	Year 1	Year 2	Year 3	Year 4	Year 5	Year 6
Account 1	$30,000	$0	$0	$0	$0	$0
Account 2	$0	$30,000	$0	$0	$0	$0
Account 3	$0	$0	$30,000	$0	$0	$0
Account 4	$0	$0	$0	$30,000	$0	$0
Account 5	$0	$0	$0	$0	$30,000	$0
Account 6	$0	$0	$0	$0	$0	$30,000
TOTAL	$30,000	$30,000	$30,000	$30,000	$30,000	$30,000

SCENARIO #2

	Year 1	Year 2	Year 3	Year 4	Year 5	Year 6
Account 1	$30,000	$30,000	$30,000	$30,000	$30,000	$30,000
Account 2	$0	$30,000	$30,000	$30,000	$30,000	$30,000
Account 3	$0	$0	$30,000	$30,000	$30,000	$30,000
Account 4	$0	$0	$0	$30,000	$30,000	$30,000
Account 5	$0	$0	$0	$0	$30,000	$30,000
Account 6	$0	$0	$0	$0	$0	$30,000
TOTAL	$30,000	$60,000	$90,000	$120,000	$150,000	$180,000

SCENARIO #3

	Year 1	Year 2	Year 3	Year 4	Year 5	Year 6
Account 1	$30,000	$30,000	$60,000	$60,000	$60,000	$60,000
Account 2	$0	$30,000	$30,000	$60,000	$60,000	$60,000
Account 3	$0	$0	$30,000	$30,000	$60,000	$60,000
Account 4	$0	$0	$0	$30,000	$30,000	$60,000
Account 5	$0	$0	$0	$0	$30,000	$30,000
Account 6	$0	$0	$0	$0	$0	$30,000
TOTAL	$30,000	$60,000	$120,000	$180,000	$240,000	$300,000

The key here is: ***Pubic Sector Selling is a Long Term Proposition!*** If your comp plan rewards you for growing accounts and additional downstream sales, public sector can be very rewarding! These are the main issues with regard to your company, now lets take a look at yourself.

Your Family Situation

What on earth could your family situation have to do with selling to government? Perhaps nothing. But there are a few circumstances that can have a great deal of effect on your ability to be successful selling to government.

The first circumstance has to do with something mentioned earlier. *Pubic Sector Selling is a Long Term Proposition.* As we have discussed in previous sections, the rewards of selling to public sector can be great. But the ramp-up time may be a good bit longer than in other vertical markets. So it is important that your family's cash flow situation is such that you can meet all of your financial obligations on your base salary alone long enough to get your business built. If you cannot handle this, you may be destined for disaster.

Picture a jet airplane that requires a minimum of 2,000 feet to take off. The pilot will probably demand at least a 2,500-foot runway to feel comfortable. Why? Because sometimes things do not work out exactly as planned. Maybe the wind changes, or the engine is a little slow to build speed, or the cargo is a little heavier than expected. So if he has a 2,500-foot runway, the jet builds speed, and right around the 2,000-foot mark the plane leaves the ground. Now picture the same jet on a 1,000-foot runway. The jet engines roar, it rolls down the runway, and right about the time it is rolling along at about 200 MPH, the runway ends at a ditch, a highway, and a row of buildings. In the example of the jet plane, there is an explosion, the plane is destroyed, and people die. If this is you trying to build a government client list, your career has exploded and your family is in financial stress. You must make sure that you have enough runway to take off!

As always, there are exceptions to this. The first is if you have no family and few obligations. If you feel lucky and think you can get the plane off the ground in 1,500 or 1,000 feet, you may be willing to risk it. When you are young and single, it is easier to recover from a disaster like this. If you lose your brand new car and have to give up the European tour you had scheduled, that is not too bad. It is different when you are risking your kid's college fund. The second exception is when you have the opportunity to take over a public sector territory that has an existing customer base that you can begin selling re-order business to right away. This is an entirely different situation. In this situation, you can start bringing in excellent commissions right away. But beware! If you are offered a position like this, it is assuming that someone else has built this business. So if someone else has this great territory that amounts to a highly profitable annuity business, why did he or she leave? Make sure the position was vacated due to a promotion, retirement, or some other event that happens to highly successful sales pros. This goes for any position you are offered.

The second circumstance is not very common, but is worth mentioning, as there are some situations in which it does present itself. This situation is when you or a family member is actively involved in politics or the government bureaucracy (we will talk more about these distinctions later). Most government agencies have very strict procurement rules regarding doing business with family members connected to the organization. If your spouse is the Assistant Director of the Department of Corrections and your company is trying to sell food services to the prison system, you may have a problem. There is a common misperception that this type of association would give you the inside track and make your sale a sure thing. But in most states there are very strict rules about conflicts of interest and you will not be able to participate in this sale. Obviously there are a few exceptions to this rule also. Some state, county, and city governments are more scrupulous regarding conflicts of interest than others. And if you have been around the business for a while you also know that there are a few that are, shall we say, "somewhat less scrupulous" than others. If you are dealing with the small minority of organizations who do operate in this less than ethical manner, you don't need this book anyway as you are playing a completely different game.

Your Selling Style

Most sales professionals today have been through at least one formal sales training program. Many of today's sales pros have been through several formal programs. In addition to formal training, most of us have read dozens of books on sales and have been properly or improperly mentored by other reps. We have heard all the old platitudes: "it's a numbers game", "its how bad you want it", "its all about qualifying", "its all timing", "its all about relationships", etc. Many of the formal methodologies attempt to reduce selling to a standardized process. They offer a gigantic spreadsheet with multiple "steps" in the sales process along with descriptions, instructions, and little check boxes to make sure you follow all the steps. All you have to do is follow the steps in order and make sure you check the boxes and VOILA, you make your number! Okay, so maybe you noticed this is another one of my pet peeves. I do not believe you can reduce selling to a step-by-step process. I think you need some sort of system to keep organized and keep on track, but selling is a very personal activity. It has to be. That is what it is. It is based on personal contact. Otherwise none of us would be employed. Companies would just have websites and catalogs so customers could order products and services from the comfort of their offices. But that is not how it works. Selling involves people interacting with other people. And since selling is a personal activity, every sales activity is unique based on the people involved. Every selling professional has his or her own unique style. Some of these styles are better suited to selling in the public sector than others. That does not mean there is no room for several styles within public sector sales. There certainly is room for a wide variety of styles (as well as personality types). But some are a natural fit while others need to either emphasize or de-emphasize particular aspects of their style. Lets take look at some of these styles and how well they fit into the public sector selling world.

The Enthusiast

Some sales pros are very excited. That is their style. They are just bubbling over with enthusiasm for their product or service. They are so excited and enthusiastic that this enthusiasm runs over and begins to infect their prospects. I have seen people who are very good at this. It is like the prospects are catching a fever. They get so anxious to buy that we sometimes have to slow them down and make sure they don't go overboard and order more than they need (which they would regret later). It is a truly amazing thing to watch, but not many salespeople can pull this off. In fact if it is something you are trying to "pull off", it won't work. It has to be a natural part of you. While this style is fantastic, it may have limited effect in long public sector sales cycles where there is often very controlled access to decision makers. Don't get me wrong. Enthusiasm for your company, product, and service still must be there. But the ecstatic fever pitch of excitement simply cannot be maintained throughout the sales cycle. Even if the sales pro can maintain it, the prospects cannot. So if you are this type of salesperson, you need to temper your energy level and pace yourself for the long run. Use your enthusiasm to be sure. But use it during presentations, corporate visits, or reference calls. You will have to tweak your style, but you can adjust to make it fit public sector.

The Pit Bull

Some salespeople like to push their prospect, control him, and drive the sales cycle. These salespeople tend to be extremely aggressive and border on being pushy. They take charge and basically tell the prospect what product or service is needed, when it should be purchased, and in what quantity. These are the take-charge types. They tend to be very impatient and on occasion almost a bit rude. But sales managers generally like these reps. Why? Because when the sales manager needs to pull in that last $100,000 in revenue at the last minute to make her quarter, she knows this guy will squeeze it out of one of his customers somehow. But when it comes to public sector, these guys are dead in the water. They have trouble following the process and do not have the patience to work the long sales cycles. If this is you, you may want to think long and hard about devoting your time to public sector.

The Advisor

These sales pros act as friend, advisor, and shoulder to cry on to their customers. They listen, empathize, and "feel their pain". The customers tell these sales reps about everything from the new budget initiative to their last PTA meeting. These people are the ones who amaze all of us during account reviews. You know the drill. Every one gets together with the sales manager and a regional director. The reps all take turns discussing your top 5, 10, or 15 accounts. The "Advisor" sales rep is the one who will have the most unbelievable amount of detailed information on almost everyone in the account! They know how old everyone is, how many kids they have, who is bucking for what promotion, who was just passed over, who gets along, who does not, and even who is romantically involved! I am not this type of salesperson but I am absolutely in awe of them. I have worked with several of these people and am always amazed by them. This style of selling works well in public sector provided the salesperson also has the attention to detail for the nuts and bolts of the process.

The Consultant

Some sales people are naturally consultative in nature. These sales pros are often viewed by customers as the experts. Their approach is calm, professional, and pleasant. They are persistent without being aggressive. They are very consistent and patient. This style generally utilizes the approach of an expert coming in to uncover information, collect data, assess the problem, and make an informed recommendation. These people tend to be process oriented and have no problem navigating the rule-driven government procurement process. This style is particularly well suited to selling in the public sector. If this is you, you may have what it takes to be very successful selling to government.

CHAPTER IV

Is it True That?

When I left the military, we moved to a city that happened to be the state capitol. As I neared the completion of my college degree, I wanted an accounting job and the only opportunities in town were with the state government. I remember being told on a very regular basis "you can't get on with the state unless you know someone there". I applied for several positions and took the appropriate civil service exams. Within a few months I had an excellent job working for a large state agency. I managed to "get on with the state" without knowing anyone there. The information I was given (all by people who did not work for the state) was wrong. Many people with little or no actual knowledge of government have some commonly held but absolutely incorrect ideas about government and selling to government. So lets look at some of the commonly held ideas and find out how true they are.

You Cannot Get a Government Contract Unless You Know Someone

This is something I hear all the time. “You closed that deal with the city, who do you know over there?” There is a very common perception that personal connections are required to do business with governments. Nothing could be further from the truth! As we will discuss later, most governments go to almost ridiculous extremes to make sure purchases are fair and unbiased. Government officials generally do not have the ability within purchasing rules to award contracts to friends. Are there some occasions where government officials manipulate the rules to favor vendors they have personal relationships with? Of course there are. You can always find a few examples of some underhanded activity in government. You may also find this sort of thing to be more prevalent in certain geographic areas. But in most government entities, throughout most of the country, this is not the norm.

It is important however for you or your firm to be known as a reliable supplier to government agencies. Government references are often a requirement and a long track record of government work is very helpful. So although you do not need to "know someone" it is important and certainly appropriate for the government buyer to feel more comfortable if they know you or your reputation as a government product or service provider.

Governments Are Corrupt

There are many commonly believed stereotypes regarding public sector procurement. One of those stereotypes involves the image of public officials pulling strings and awarding contracts in exchange for cash or other types of payoffs. It has been a long held theory that government was somehow much less open and more corruptible than the private sector. This view has unfortunately been disproved lately thanks to several large and previously respectable firms in industries such as accounting, energy, and mutual funds. Greed and corruption are human weaknesses, not government weaknesses. Governments are full of people. Some people are honest and some are not. Some dishonest people work their way into the public sector just as they do into the private sector. If anything, it is more difficult to engage in corruption in the public sector given the level of oversight most governments are subject to. It would be difficult to find government corruption on the scale of some of the scandals we have seen in the private sector in recent years.

Yes, there are occasional high profile cases of government corruption. One Friday evening I was stuffing envelopes while watching the local evening news. I glanced up and saw something that grabbed my attention. It was a picture of the face of a local public official I was planning to meet with in the near future. I had not been listening to what the newscaster had said up to that point. So I stopped what I was doing and paid close attention in order to find out what the report was about. At that moment the newscast cut to a video of the public official being led away in handcuffs! He had been arrested on corruption charges. He had taken cash bribes in exchange for awarding contracts to vendors. Needless to say, I never had the meeting! My sales manager called me wanting to know if I had managed to get the contract signed before the arrest (sales managers are funny guys). Fortunately this type of corruption is not the norm. But it does occur and is more common in some parts of the country than others. Hopefully you can work your entire career without ever running into this sort of thing. But if you ever do, just disqualify the prospect and move on. Do not deal with these people at all!

Governments Are Inefficient

Yes, this one is true. Governments are less efficient than most private firms. But that is fine. They should not be as efficient as private companies. Why? The reason is that governmental agencies are not designed with efficiency as their primary objective. This is an area of misunderstanding that causes a great deal of frustration for business people selling into government. The procurement process for most government agencies seems to be constructed to deliberately make it as difficult as possible. I have been working with governments for years, understand the process well, and at times it still drives me nuts! But if you understand the rationale behind this deliberate complexity, it may help you to deal with it more effectively.

Think for a minute what it is like to sell to a small privately owned business, Frank's Widgets. You work with Frank and you sell him on your product or service. You then discuss price, payment terms, etc. You sign the deal and you are done! Why is it so easy? Because it is Frank's company. Frank does not have to answer to anyone. When he writes the check, that is Frank's money.

Now think about your dealings with a corporation, Western Widgets Incorporated. If your product or service costs any substantial amount, you generally have more than one person involved in the sales cycle (for large procurements there is often a selection committee). Once you sell them on your idea, there may have to be board approval before moving ahead. Then the corporate counsel will have to review the contracts, etc. It is more complex because the executives are now spending other people's money. They are responsible to the Western Widgets shareholders! These shareholders have invested in the company, and the board and executives must answer to them. This is much less efficient than dealing with a one-owner company, but it has to be.

Now imagine you are selling to the City of Widgetville. Suddenly things become much more complex, the rules seem insurmountable, and the timeframe is out of sight. Why? Because the city officials are answerable to the taxpayers. Think about it for a moment. The corporate executives are answerable to a group of people who voluntarily invested their money in the company. The city officials are answerable to people from whom money had been taken by law and against their will if necessary. I have heard taxes described as "involuntary contributions". If I do not like the way Western Widgets, Inc. handles the business, I will just sell the stock. But when there is an entity with the power to make laws to forcibly take money from me, they must conform to a higher standard of due diligence. Government officials are trustees of public funds. They must take much greater care when they spend taxpayer's money. So it is not the most efficient way to operate, but efficiency is not the goal.

Governments Have No Accountability

I once worked in the accounting department of a large state agency. I had some friends who worked in the private sector in a variety of industries. One time during a conversation they began to comment on what they perceived as a lack of accountability in the public sector. They would talk about shareholder accountability as well as their "Big Eight" audits (at that time there were eight major accounting firms and they primarily engaged in accounting and auditing). So I in turn told them about my agency. We also by law had an annual audit from a Big Eight firm. But we also underwent an audit from the State Auditor's Office. This included not only a financial audit, but compliance and performance audits as well. The Auditor was an elected position (often seen as a stepping stone to Attorney General then Governor). Given the political nature of the office, these guys came in digging hard to find anything that would remotely look like inefficiency or impropriety. These auditors were in our offices literally six months out of the year. As if the Big Eight and the State were not enough, the Feds also got involved. We underwent annual audits by two Federal agencies from whom we received large amounts of funding. We also hosted several limited scope annual audits from other federal and state agencies regarding the particular funds they sent us. Oh, and there was also a legislative oversight committee that would order occasional spot audits whenever they saw fit!

Public sector also has the added dimension of visibility. Almost everything that is done in a government agency is considered open as a public record. There is not much room to hide. Even activities that are not unethical may be interpreted and reported that way. I will give you another real life example.

I worked for a company that utilized a corporate credit card. The card was issued in the employees' names and the bills came directly to us. When we used the card for an expense (such as a hotel room) we would take the receipt and file it in our weekly expense report for reimbursement. When the credit card bills came to us, we paid the bills out of our personal checking accounts. I was caught out holiday shopping once and did not have my regular credit card, so I used the corporate card. I simply did not file for reimbursement for the personal items I purchased so the company did not incur the expense. A few weeks later our AP department informed me that they periodically reconcile expense reports to the credit card reports and that I should not use the corporate card for anything that I was not going to put on my expense report. It fouled up their reports. I apologized and did not do it again. End of story. But an almost identical situation occurred with a city employee (we will call him Bill Smith). Bill had family in from out of town for a wedding. He took a rather large party of people out to dinner, only to find out at the end of the meal they did not accept the particular personal credit card he carried. So he used the city corporate card and assumed that since he was not going to request reimbursement and just pay it himself, there would be no problem. But the city did the same type of reconciliation as my company. It fouled up their reports so they told Bill not to do it again. But since it was all public record, a newspaper reporter got a hold of it. A couple of weeks later this poor guy's picture was on the front page of the newspaper with a headline that read "Bill Jones Caught Misappropriating City Funds". The story went on to say that he used city funds to treat family and friends to a "lavish" dinner. It named the restaurant and even listed the items ordered (which of course included steak, lobster, beer, wine, Champaign, and a generous tip). The story was completely misleading. Bill did not spend one penny of the city's money. He had to explain the entire thing to the newspaper and about a week later they printed a correction, two sentences long, in small type, on page eight.

If anyone starts in with the old mantra about no accountability in the public sector, send them to me!

You Need to Contribute to a Campaign to get a Government Contract

This seldom has any impact on most government procurements. One reason is the majority of procurements involve very little input from elected officials. Civil servants in the purchasing agency generally handle everyday procurements (more about the players involved later). Once again, there are exceptions. Elected officials will generally get involved for any of the following reasons:

#1 – The dollar amount of the procurement is high.

#2 – It involves a project of particular interest to the official (an initiative he or she has worked on, etc.)

#3 – The procurement is politically charged for some reason.

#4 – There is a lot of publicity (good or bad) connected to the procurement.

Keep in mind that campaign contributions often will buy access to some elected officials. But this can be a very costly process as there are often several officials involved in the high-dollar, high profile opportunities. Unless you are very politically involved and know the turf well, do not do this on your own. If you are moving into opportunities that have a high level of involvement from elected officials it may well be worth the investment to contract with a lobbyist to guide you through the process.

You Have to be a Minority Business to get a Government Contract

So do you have to be a minority to sell to government? Absolutely not. A lot has been discussed in the last several years regarding minority owned businesses selling to the public sector. Many people feel very strongly about this subject on both sides of the aisle. It is very important to understand this factor with regard to the government procurement process. It is not important because it is a determining factor in your ability to sell to government. It is important that you understand it because you will find this issue present in most government procurements. So lets first discuss just what it is.

Most government agencies have implemented special considerations into their procurement rules regarding businesses that are considered a Minority-Owned Business Enterprise or a Woman-Owned Business Enterprise. These are often labeled as MBE/WBE. These acronyms are commonly pronounced "Meebie-Weebie". I do not recommend using this term with your customer as some people may think you do not take the program seriously and are being flippant. Most governments have clearly defined criteria for what constitutes a MBE/WBE. Many organizations simply look at the ownership percentage. If 51% or more of the ownership is an ethnic minority they qualify as a MBE. If 51% or more of the ownership is female, they qualify as a WBE. Some agencies may have additional requirements. The programs generally work in one of two ways. Many agencies select vendors based on points awarded. The vendor will receive points for the applicability of references, stability of the company, the price being quoted, etc. In this case, the agencies may choose to award extra points for MBE/WBEs. In some agencies if the bids are strictly price driven, they may use a formula to adjust the quoted price for the purpose of giving the MBE/WBE an advantage. It is somewhat like the process of awarding extra points on a postal exam if the applicant is a veteran (I actually don't know if the Postal Service still does this). Government agencies may also have a goal that specifies each department do some percentage of their contracts with MBE/WBEs. If this is the case, make sure you do not use the term "quota" with your prospect. If so, you will risk really upsetting some people. Government procurement people will use terms such as "goal" or "target". Remember, you cannot be sure if the government employees you are working with are conservatives or liberals. And often you will be working with a mix of both throughout any given sales cycle. It is very important to understand that not all government organizations or people in these organizations feel the same way about MBE/WBE. Some take it extremely seriously, view it as a moral imperative, and feel it is matter of social justice. Some may view it as left wing social engineering bordering on Marxism. Some just view it as more paperwork and red tape. Many have a mix of these feelings to varying degrees. But regardless of how they feel about it, every agency will dot the I's and cross the T's on this. If it is part of the process, it will be followed. So now that you know what MBE/ WBE is, how important is it?

The impact of MBE/WBE programs will vary between agencies as well as individual sales cycles. If you are trying to do business with a city government and that city has a disproportionately high minority population, they will most likely have very high targets for MBE/WBE contracts. Another factor has to do with where a particular organization stands with regard to attainment of their targets. If an agency is currently far below their target percentage or dollar amount and has been receiving bad publicity for it in the local media, MBE/WBE will be a factor. However, if you are doing business with a large organization in an urban area, they may have no problem reaching their targets every year and it may be no factor whatsoever. In my experience selling to state and local government from the West Coast to the East Coast, it is usually not a major factor. It is simply one part of a large package of benefits being offered by the various vendors.

But what if you feel MBE/ WBE is a factor and your company is not a MBE/WBE? If your company is engaging in some type of contracting work (building roads, designing computer systems, removing snow) you can often sub-contract a portion of the work to a MBE/WBE. There is another option, but it should be used with caution. Once MBE/WBE programs began, it did not take long for some firms to figure out a "workaround". It goes like this. A firm wants to do business with a MBE/WBE intensive government. But the firm cannot qualify as a MBE/WBE. So they start another firm and bring in a minority or woman partner and make them a 51% owner. Or they find a MBE/WBE firm and come to an arrangement with them. The new MBE/WBE firm then bids on the contract as a qualified MBE/WBE. Once they win the business, they sub-contract most of the work back to the original non-MBE/WBE firm. The MBE/WBE keeps a fair-size cut of the deal in exchange for being the "front man". In most cases this is absolutely legal, even if it sounds a little shady. If you decide to bid this way, make sure it meets the agency's requirements. Also, make sure you understand the attitude of that agency. If this agency takes the spirit of MBE/WBE to heart, they will know what you are doing and will find a way to disqualify you. If the agency is just following the rules because they have to and just see MBE/WBE as another check box on their to-do list, you should be okay.

The best approach is usually to bid directly and sub contract to a MBE/WBE.

Government Employees are Inefficient

I once believed this fable myself. Contrary to my parent's urging I did not go to college after high school. I had other plans and eventually ended up in the military. After the service I worked selling business equipment. Several of my prospects were government agencies. I thought this was a rather lazy, un-motivated, and inefficient group of people. I complained incessantly about them. While I was selling I was going to school at night earning my Accounting degree. I could not wait to start my Accounting career and get out of the selling racket and away from those government customers. But then as fate would have it, when I received my degree the only accounting job I could find was a government job! I could not believe how slowly the people around me worked. They seemed to just be "doing their time". But then something very enlightening happened. I took a part-time evening job at a local division of a large national corporation. There were many other government employees "moonlighting" at this company. Some were even people I knew from my day job. But there was something very different. The same employees who seemed to move in slow motion during the day in their government jobs were on high speed at the company on night shift! They were moving quickly. They exhibited a great degree of energy, motivation, and creativity! Then suddenly it all clicked. The people working in government were not different. The system was different!

People are the same everywhere. Workers will engage in the type of behavior they are rewarded for. They will avoid engaging in the type of behavior they are penalized for. Most government work is process driven. This is the way it should be. Government is not a profit-oriented organization. Civil servants are custodians of other people's money (yours and mine). Because of this they are required to operate within what are often very narrowly prescribed parameters. Achieving an end result faster with lower cost is not something that is rewarded if the processes are not followed properly. In fact, a government employee can be severely penalized for failing to follow some procedures and processes. These moonlighting government employees were rewarded on their private sector job while taking orders over the phone if they could upsell and convince the customer to purchase a few additional products along with their order. Imagine your county clerk trying to "upsell" when you are paying your property tax!

Government Attracts the "Dim Bulbs"

So who would want to work for government anyway? Certainly the most skilled professionals in the field would want to ply their trade elsewhere. Why would anyone want to settle for the mediocrity of "government work" in the face of the siren song of the astronomical compensation packages of Corporate America? Certainly the people working for government are the "dim bulbs", right? Wrong, wrong, wrong.

As I mentioned earlier, when I first started working for a large state agency I expected the worst. But slowly I started to discover a very large number of extremely bright people working in government. They were attracted to government work for a variety of reasons. One of these reasons was professional interest.

I was at a social function with a large number of state employees. I found myself in a conversation with an interesting fellow. He mentioned that he worked for the State Department of Transportation. I asked what he did and he told me he was an archeologist. I commented that archaeology must have been a very interesting major in college, but asked him what his job was for the department. He showed me his Department of Transportation business card that listed his job title as Senior Archeologist! He supervised an entire team of archeologists. I was fascinated. I had to question him about this situation. As it turns out, there are several laws relating to maintaining the integrity of archeological sites. This is particularly true with regard to Native American villages and burial sites. So when the State Department of Transportation needs to start tearing into a riverbank to lay a bridge foundation or blasting into the side of a mountain for a tunnel, an archeologist has to make sure there is no evidence of a potential archeological find. And if there is, they start a "dig". He then introduced me to several of his co-workers. Up until that night I had never met an archeologist. And at this party of government employees I met five! Here were a group of highly skilled and well-trained professionals. They were making a reasonable living, in a steady job, with excellent benefits. Where else could they actively practice their craft? A typical option for them would be tramping around in a South American jungle or African dessert without their family for subsistence wages!

There are many professional opportunities in government that are scarce or simply do not exist in the private sector. Government is the natural choice for most highly skilled professionals in fields such as criminal justice, forestry, civil engineering, urban planning, and public health.

Many professionals enter government for the experience and level of responsibility available. It is typical for a professional in government to be appointed to a position of much greater responsibility than someone at a similar point in their career would be in the private sector. This is particularly attractive to young professionals interested in building fine careers. I knew an attorney working for the state government who by virtue of representing a state agency had the opportunity to bring arguments to the U.S. Supreme Court on two occasions! How many young attorneys at even the most exclusive Manhattan law firms ever get an opportunity like that?

And believe it or not, many people do work in the public sector out of a sense of public service. They believe that what they are doing is important (and it is). Yes, there really are a large number of people in government who are driven out of a sense of duty and ideals, not just money.

You will find quite a mix of people working in government. But remember that it is a mix. They are not all cut from the same cloth. Jumping to conclusions about the people you are dealing with in a government organization is a big mistake.

CHAPTER V

Who is Involved in the Government Sales Cycle and What Motivates Them?

Elected Executives

In most governments the elected executive functions as the CEO of that government. In a state government he/she is the Governor. At the county level he/she may be called a Commissioner or County Executive. At the municipal level there is generally a Mayor. In some cities there may also be a Mayor and a City Manager. This relationship is similar to the relationship between a Chief Executive Officer and a Chief Operations Officer.

Depending on your product or service the executive may or may not be involved in your sales cycle. This depends a good bit on the price and nature of your offering. The executive often needs to at least sign-off on purchases over a certain size. But he/she will almost always have involvement if it is a procurement or contract that has any possibility at all of receiving publicity (good or bad).

The elected executive may want to be involved directly, but more often than not, the executive will have advisors reporting to him or her. If you are involved in a competitive sales cycle, the elected executive may not be involved in the selection at all, but may reserve veto or override authority. By the time there is an actual procurement process in place, the Mayor or Commissioner has most likely decided if they wish to be involved or not. Just make sure that if they have delegated, the delegates have the authority to decide, not just recommend.

If they want to meet with the sales reps, they will meet with all of them. If they do not want to meet with any, they will not. You can ask, and you should. But understand, if they decide to meet with you they will almost always meet with your competitors also. If they refuse to meet with you, they are most likely not meeting with your competitors either. Most government procurement rules do not allow a public official to meet with a vendor unless they meet with all vendors. Many sales courses and sales training methodologies will tell you that if you cannot get a meeting with the C-level decision maker you should disqualify the opportunity. If you choose to follow the advice of many sales trainers and walk away, you will simply be conceding the business to another vendor who has also been refused access, but understands the public sector procurement process well enough to stick it out and win the business.

Elected Executives are politicians. As mentioned before, public sector employees are goal oriented and competitive. For an elected official (politician) the goal is generally one of two things:

- To be re-elected to the current office

- To run for election to a higher office

So what are an elected official's "hot-buttons", "critical needs", "pain points", "key drivers", etc.? The particulars differ from time to time and place to place. In general they make decisions based on whatever will help them achieve their goals or what will minimize the risk of something interfering with the accomplishment of their goals. So the areas you as a sales rep need to be keyed into are what the general hot button issues are in that city or county. Is it early in the mayor's term or late? If it is early, the mayor is most likely focused on accomplishing his/her goals and making progress. The other party just got stomped and they are licking their wounds. If they oppose the new mayor now it will be viewed as "sour grapes". The ousted party will just lie in wait. The mayor has just been elected and wants to get things done and deliver. This is the time to push new technology and innovative solutions that will modernize city services and improve customer service to the citizens.

If it is late in the mayor's term, things are different. The elections are just around the corner. The honeymoon is long over. Enough time has passed for several things to happen that have caused some number of the citizenry to be disenchanted with the mayor (regardless of whether or not the mayor had anything to do with them). The opposition party is looking for anything that looks remotely like scandal, negligence, or poor judgment. At this point the mayor's office will be operating defensively. Risk aversion will be the prime directive. They are not about to sink a large sum of money into anything innovative and untried. This may not only swing their favor away from you and toward your competitors, but may stop the procurement process altogether. It is not that they do not understand what you are offering. They may totally understand that what you are selling really poses no risk. But if they think there may be the possibility that acting on your proposal could be perceived or represented as being any sort of folly, you are dead in the water. And if what you are doing could in any way be perceived in even the most remote fashion as anything but above board, pack your bags and head home. You are done. The best approach at this stage of an executive's term is to offer something that has little risk, offers a very quick and measurable cost savings, and/or will provide a very visible and popular benefit to the citizens (i.e. voters).

Appointed Executives

Appointed executives are generally executives who head either departments of the parent government (county department of parks, state health department, etc.), or semi-autonomous agencies (port authority, water district, etc.). It is important to note that some of these types of positions may be elected and some appointed. This can vary from place to place. The Chief of Police may be an appointed position in one city and an elected position in another.

Their functions are very much like a CEO in the case of an autonomous agency. In the case of a department they function more like a VP reporting to the CEO. For example, in the private sector the VP of marketing will make most decisions regarding advertising contracts and the like. But they still are answerable to the CEO.

The general process for appointing people to these positions is that the elected official (governor, mayor, etc.) announces the person for appointment and they need to be confirmed by a representative body (senate, representatives, city council, etc.). So the person cannot simply be a favorite of the elected executive, he/she must also engender favor or at least neutrality from the representative body to confirm them.

While elected officials tend to be somewhat similar (politicians), there are some different types of appointed officials.

- **Politicians**: Some appointed officials are politicians as are elected officials. They may have held elected office in the past and this may be a higher profile position that will lead to a higher elected office in the future. An example is a city mayor later appointed by the governor as the head of the State Health Department to be followed by a campaign for State Attorney General. This group may or may not know much about the actual "business" of the department they are appointed to head. These people are generally appointed because of personal or political relationships with the appointing official. They are trusted political partners who will help to carry out the agenda of the elected executive.

- **Political Insiders**: These are the people who do not run for office themselves, but are very involved in the political process. They work on campaigns, assist elected officials, conduct fundraisers, help build coalitions of supporters, or donate sums of money themselves. In essence they are "true believers" in a particular candidate, political issue, or political party. They are often appointed to these positions for the same reasons as the politicians, but sometimes also as a reward for a job well done on a campaign.

- **Political Professionals**: This group is generally appointed to positions where their professional and/or technical expertise is required to run the organization and they also will be required to drive policy. An example may be the chief engineer of a department of public works. The job may require that the director be a civil engineer by training. Another may be the position of chief counsel or attorney general, both requiring the holder of those positions to be an attorney. These positions are given to politically connected professionals who also fit the educational/vocational requirements of the position
- **Technocrats**: These are the people who are appointed to a position because they have the experience, skills, and abilities to actually run the organization or department regardless of political history. In fact, these people often are not very politically oriented at all and may be known to the appointing executive by reputation only. Examples here may be a Chief Information Officer who is a retired

CIO from private industry or a Director of Economic Development who previously was the head economist for a large bank.

In any case, appointed officials are differentiated from elected officials in a very major way. Their allegiance is not to the voters, but to the politician who appointed them. The political professional and particularly the technocrats have less allegiance as they often have many career options outside politics. This is good in that they often are more willing to listen to you, think outside the box, and take a calculated risk. But they also are often more loosely connected and may not have the political clout to push a particular procurement through the process.

The hot buttons for the more politically oriented appointees are generally the same ones of their appointing elected officials. Whatever makes their benefactor look good is what makes them happy. By the way, is this any different than dealing with the young VP who is the CEO's favorite?

Elected Representatives

These people are also politicians. They function in the legislative role. They generally are considered representatives of specific geographical areas within the governmental entity. At the state level they are state representatives or state senators from different districts. At the county level they are generally a Board of Commissioners (in New Jersey they are called a Board of Chosen Freeholders) representing different regions or districts. At the municipal level is a City Council or Board of Alderman with the members representing different wards or boroughs.

They have many of the same concerns and issues as the elected executives. But they are more coalition-oriented. Their concerns are split between their own political welfare and the success of the party. This can often put them in difficult positions. For example, a particular city councilman's party may be working hard to get approval for a new highway extension. But that extension may be forcing the removal of several popular family businesses in that councilman's ward. The key here is to understand what is going on in the community. Do not assume all members of the same party are on the same side of every issue. This guy may need the support of his party, but he needs the vote of his constituents even more.

Bureaucrats

Bureaucrats are the managers who actually run the machinery of a government. They are the managers responsible for collecting the taxes, maintaining the parks, repairing the roads, buying the police cars, issuing license plates and managing the hundreds or thousands of other daily functions of a governmental agency. These are the career government managers. They were here doing their job when the last Republican governor was in office, and the two Democrats before him, and the Republican before that. These folks have political preferences like everyone else, but generally keep it out of the office. They are public servants and are there to get the job done. Besides, they know the political climate will change many times throughout their careers. An example of some of these types of positions might be the Finance Director, County Engineer, IT Director, or Director of Corrections. These people have worked their way up through the system much as someone would in a regular private sector corporation. Most begin as lower level civil servants. You will find some who literally started in the mailroom. Purchasing decisions are often made at this level. These folks may have to go to the elected officials for their annual budget approvals, but the spending of their operating budget is generally up to them within the constraints of procurement rules (more about that later).

Bureaucrats generally just want to climb the career ladder as far as they can until retirement. This can mean moving up in the same agency (Assistant Director to Director) or moving to a higher position in a different agency or entity. It is not unusual for an experienced bureaucrat in a county government to move to a position at a large city, etc.

Civil Servants

These are the rank and file employees. They report to the bureaucrats. And like the bureaucrats, their careers will span many political administrations. These positions are filled either through open advertising like any private sector job, or through a formal civil service exam process. The non-professionals (i.e. no college) generally move through some sort of position and pay matrix (Clerk I, Clerk II – Level 1, Clerk II – Level 2, etc.). These people generally are not involved in the procurement process unless they are part of an evaluation team of end users. An example may be heavy equipment operators actually testing the bulldozers you are proposing.

The Purchasing Officer

This one position requires special consideration. This position will generally fall under either the bureaucrat or civil servant categories mentioned above. This position in a government agency is not the same as a buyer in a private sector firm. They do not have anything to do with the selection of vendors, products, pricing, or any normal sales decisions. They also do not have the power to help you win the deal. But they can kill your sale in a heartbeat! You cannot wine and dine these people as you would a buyer in a private company. This person is not a buyer. This person has one duty and one only; to make sure all purchasing rules are followed to the letter of the law! If all proposals are to be received on February 10th at 4:15 PM, this is the person who will disqualify you if yours shows up at 4:16. You cannot ignore this person or bypass him/her. You can develop all the relationships you want with others in the organization, but this rule keeper will hold your feet to the fire. Treat this person's rules like the law. They often are!

As I mentioned, you cannot wine, dine, and schmooze the Purchasing Officer to get favors. However, if you go out of your way to make him/her an enemy, you will most likely be in big trouble. Governmental purchasing rules can be a nearly indecipherable maze of seemingly conflicting processes. At some point you will need the Purchasing Officer to help guide you through this endless abyss. Again, there is no need to attempt to get special treatment, helping you through the process is their job. But treat these people well. Treat them like professionals even when their words and actions do not seem to make sense to you. This is their job and this is their world. Respect that.

CHAPTER VI

How Does the Government Buying Process Work?

Most of us have been through numerous sales training classes and have read countless sales books all of which tout the importance of demanding access to "C-Level" officers. Many even advocate walking away from an opportunity if that access is not granted. Two points I would like to make here. The first is that these sales trainers and authors telling you to walk away from opportunities have already made their sale (to your management to get the training contract or to their publisher to print their book). Very few of the sales trainers whose training I have attended have ever met with the CEO or Board of Directors of our company. They tell some good stories, but I am not sure how successful any of them really were in sales (of all the sales trainers I have been exposed to, there are only a handful of them I would be inclined to buy anything from). The second point is that these guys generally know very little if anything about selling to government.

I was selling in a very competitive technology field that had several lead players. All were well known by the prospects, and most were considered to have the ability to meet the prospect's needs. Virtually every deal I was involved in was a head-to-head competition between the same 4 or 5 vendors. Between bidder's conferences and trade shows, I even came to personally know some of the sales reps working for my competitors. One of these companies in particular was very notorious for having extremely aggressive salespeople. Their sales reps were required to meet with the CEO or a board member of any company they were selling to. If the prospect had a rule against contacting the c-level team, this was considered even better. It meant to this company that since no one else had the audacity to break the rules and call on the CEO, they would have the edge. If they could not secure a meeting with the CEO, they would literally stalk the guy and try to "casually" meet him in a restaurant, at the golf club, or in the shopping mall. They tried to carry this practice over to the public sector.

We were nearing the end of a sales cycle on a reasonably large deal. Unfortunately, we were not winning. We were clearly in second place, but we were stuck. There were a couple of small requirements the prospect had that we could not meet. As you might guess, the first place company (the one with the aggressive sales tactics) found out about this and exploited the situation by convincing the prospects that these two small requirements were critical to the survival of democracy. Nine months of work and a lot of hotel and airfare expenses were going down the drain. Then something happened that could not have been sweeter.

The procurement policy in the RFP clearly stated which team members we were allowed to contact. Any contact outside that group would disqualify the vendor's proposal. Although

"Salesman X" was in the process of winning the deal, he had not yet met with the CEO equivalent at the government agency (none of the other vendors had met with him either). He was winning, but had an account review coming up with his sales manager and regional sales director. The entire sales team did this quarterly. It was something that resembled a cross between a congressional inquiry and the Spanish Inquisition. He knew he had to meet with the CEO. He tracked the guy down and met him at a local watering hole. He bought several rounds of drinks and they talked for a couple of hours. They got along very well and by all reports had a marvelous time. The next Monday an email went out to all vendors telling us that his company was disqualified from the bidding! They were thrown out on their backsides so fast they did not know what had hit them! I loved it for two reasons. First of all, I never did like those guys and felt it could not have happened to a more deserving group. And secondly, we were now in first place! The vendor sent VPs on private jets, offered free services and huge discounts, and did everything they could think of to get back into the deal. But nothing helped. They were gone and that was that.

What happened was simple. The vendor was focused on themselves and not the prospect. The vendor was busy pushing their own agenda by insisting on following their internal process that required a check in the box next to "met with CEO". But they forgot about the agenda of the prospect (which is the one that matters). And the agenda of the prospect was for the vendors to follow the prospect's process.

Government Procurement is Process Driven

There is a simple truth in government buying. Government procurement is process-driven. This is a very simple concept. But even very seasoned sales professionals forget this simple concept. It either drives or influences almost every aspect of a government sales cycle. It has to. Remember the discussions in previous sections. These people are not spending their own money. They are not spending money that shareholders have voluntarily invested in hopes of earning returns. They are spending public money that was extracted from the populace with or without their consent (forcibly when required). They are custodians of other people's money. Hence, they have extremely strict rules. These "processes" are there to protect the public funds. What is most important is that the process is followed and the bidding is fair. Keeping this in mind every single step of the way will not only remove a good deal of stress, but it will help you to sell better by understanding the customer's perspective.

Here is an example: Suppose you are in a deal and all seems to be going well. You have made the initial contact when you thought there was a potential fit for your product. You have spoken with several executives and elected officials at the government agency and they were very enthusiastic. You have developed what you believe to be a very good relationship. The agency has decided to move forward and the elected official tells you that they are in the process of putting it all together.

The next thing you know, you receive information from a purchasing officer that you cannot contact anyone at the agency except her and that you must respond to a formal RFP. You know that the RFP will bring all of your competitors into the deal also. You try to explain to the purchasing officer that you have already been working with the executives and they are ready to ink a deal with you. The purchasing officer is inflexible and refuses to listen or discuss the matter. She simply recites the standard rules to you. You keep trying to contact the people you had been working with but they refuse to return your calls.

What do you do? You follow the best advice of your extensive sales training. You assume that the deal is going south. If this were a case study in one of the training courses you have been through, what would the sales trainers tell you? Simple, they would tell you that you that someone else got to the C-level people and pulled the rug out from under you. They have gained executive sponsorship and have squeezed you out of the deal. As of now, you are losing badly and are not likely to recover. So you may as well try something drastic because you now have nothing to lose.

Since none of your former contacts will return your calls, your last ditch drastic move is to contact an elected executive at the agency to plead your case (going over the heads of the contacts you had been dealing with). You do so and the executive sounds very concerned and tells you that he will look into it. The next day, one of your original contacts calls you with the following message: "What the heck are you doing? We were completely sold on your product. We went to the purchasing officer to get the paperwork together, and she told us that since your product is categorized as a security product, we require an RFP. We were not allowed to contact you. We did not know an RFP would be required for this, but it was no big deal. We wrote the RFP so that your product would be the only one that met the requirements. We would have collected the proposals, selected your company, and then moved ahead with he deal. But since you contacted someone at the agency, the purchasing officer disqualified you from the bid!

Now we are going to have to buy that substandard product from your competitor." Then the email goes out to everyone announcing that you have been disqualified (so all your competitors can have a good laugh). You are going to have a lot of fun explaining this at your next account review.

What should have happened? The first thing is that you should have known what the procurement rules were. YOU should have discussed this with your prospect. You should know what procurement rules apply to your product. Imagine the scenario when your prospect says they want to move forward and you are able to tell them that you believe the procurement rules may require an RFP. You offer to give them a generic RFP that some of your previous customers have used to save them the time and trouble of writing one from scratch. You find out when they are going to contact the purchasing officer and you let them know that you will not be able to speak to them once the RFP process starts but that you will contact them immediately once the bids are opened and the silence rule is over. Not only arc you prepared for what happens, you are also providing value to you prospect by assisting them with their own procurement process. That is pretty impressive.

You may be saying “what”? “I am supposed to help them with their process?” That’s right! If you are in a sales cycle with high-level officials, it is because this is some sort of high profile procurement. These people are often not involved in day-to-day procurement. There may be no reason they should know much at all about their procurement policies. How much do you know about your company’s procurement policies regarding fire rating of cubicle walls and office furniture in the corporate office? Probably nothing. But there is someone in your company who does. So what the heck are you supposed to do? Three things:

#1 – Do not assume your prospect knows all of his/her own purchasing procedures.

#2 – Find out who does know all of the prospect’s purchasing procedures.

#3 – Talk to this person and find out everything they know that relates to your deal.

You can differentiate yourself and your company not just by your product and service, but also by demonstrating your knowledge of the prospect's process and your ability and willingness to follow that process.

Government Procurement Methods

We briefly touched on the concept of the RFP earlier. But there are actually several different methods of purchasing used by government. These include but are not limited to:

- Open Bid
- Blanket Contract
- State Contract
- GSA
- Sole Source Contract
- RFP

Open Bid

This is a common method of procurement used extensively for purchases of reasonably standardized products and services. For example, a city may purchase road salt for de-icing the roads. It is a standardized commodity and purchased in bulk. The city will post a notification and requirements to the public (often in a local newspaper and now on the city's website). This is often referred to as a "bid letting". They "let" the bid. This type of bid has very straightforward and easy to understand requirements. They will want something like X number of metric tons of grade X salt. Anyone wanting the business will submit a sealed bid. There is a formal bid opening where all the bids are read. Points are awarded based on price and other criteria. Then a vendor is selected. Obviously this varies from place to place, but that is the general idea. Prospective vendors usually need to be on the City's approved bidder's list. This should not be overly difficult nor expensive to do. You will have to submit some paperwork.

This usually involves demonstrating that your company is a legal entity, is financially sound, is properly insured, and is bondable.

Blanket Contract

This is sometimes called a blanket PO (purchase order). This is used for something that does not need to be purchased all at once, but does not require a new bid for every incremental purchase. For example, assume a State Department of Transportation (DOT) is planning to widen a segment of highway. This project will involve a lot of digging and destruction of the natural plant growth required to prevent erosion. So the DOT will have to plant grass seed along the entire stretch of road. They estimate how much they will need and let a bid for the entire amount. Suppose the total accepted bid comes to $100,000. They award the vendor a blanket contract. This means that the DOT then can order incremental amounts up to the $100,000 amount at the quoted price. So they may need $12,000 of seed in month one of the project. So they simply order $12,000 worth. They may need none in months two and three. Then in month four they may need $20,000 worth, so they order that. This allows the government agency to order what they need as they go along without having to let a bid every time.

State Contract

I use the term State Contract, as that is most common. But many large cities and counties manage their own contract programs also. What this means is that the vendor executes an actual contract with the State agreeing to sell their products or services at a specified price for a specific period. The vendor provides a price list or schedule and the State then can order off that contract. In many states, cities, counties, and schools can purchase off the state contract. The important thing about this type of contract is that it often relieves the government agency of the burdensome requirements of the RFP process. If the government agency already knows what product or service they want, this is a very welcome benefit. And if the product or service they want is yours, it will be a welcome benefit for you!

GSA

GSA stands for the General Services Administration. This is a federal agency. The GSA schedule is the primary procurement tool for the federal government. It functions very much like the state contract does at the state level. Although this is administered by a federal government agency and is primarily for federal procurement, there is some state and local applicability. Fairly recent changes in the law give most state and local governments the option of purchasing off the GSA schedule. Some take advantage of this, and some don't. If you are selling into a state account that makes use of the GSA schedule, your company should be on it. If your company is not, there are a couple of ways around it. The first is to become a subcontractor to a prime contractor who is on the GSA. The second is to allow your product or service to be sold by a company that does nothing but resell based on the GSA. These reseller companies do not carry any products of their own. They simply handle all the schedules, contracts, and other paperwork required. You sell like you normally would, but bring them in to handle the contracts. They in turn, take a percentage. If your company is not focused on government sales, this may be your best bet.

Sole-Source Contract

This is the holy grail of public sector sales. But it is rare. What the sole-source contract does is allows the government agency to bypass any of the other procurement methods mentioned (competitive bid, RFP, etc.). The agency goes straight to the vendor and executes an agreement without jumping through any of the hoops required by the other processes. "So far it sounds good, but what's the catch?" you say. Yes there is a catch. In order for the agency to make a sole-source procurement, they must conclude that your company is the only one that can provide the product or service they need.

Already you can see that this will by definition be a rare occurrence. How many products or services can you think of that are only provided by one vendor? My guess is few if any. So how could this ever be justified? There are a few ways.

One justification is made when the requirements of the procurement are so specific and unique that no one else really does offer it. This is most common when the product or service goes along with another product or service that has already been purchased. For example, an agency purchases a library of informational documents (federal environmental guidelines, corporation directories, etc.). They also may purchase an annual maintenance service that provides updates as they are available. When they need to renew the maintenance service next year, they will use a sole-source contract because that firm is the only one who provides updates of their own product. Another possibility is the case with some extremely sophisticated scientific products and services. A state university may need to install some cutting edge piece of scientific testing equipment that is made by only one very small but industry-specific technology firm in Asia. It can also occur when a vendor owns a patent for a specific product.

This may happen with a purchase by a government public health agency. They may sole-source from a pharmaceutical firm that is the only developer and patent holder on a needed vaccine.

Another justification is time and/or location. There may be several vendors capable of providing the product or service, but only one capable of doing it in the required amount of time. I experienced this situation while working in government in the Midwest. We were having unbelievable floods that year. All the rivers were overflowing their banks, roads were washing out, bridges were impassable, and people were stranded on their rooftops. We were in desperate need of sandbags. Most vendors were completely sold out that year. We did find a vendor overseas who had them in stock, and we bought direct. They were the only vendor who could provide the product within the time period we needed it. We also were in desperate need of small flat-bottom outboard boats (known as jon boats). There was no way to accept a delivery and distribute them to various locations throughout the state, so we just purchased them directly from local boat dealers nearest the location they were needed. The dealer was the only vendor able to deliver the boat the same day on location on that particular river.

Cost can be a justification also as it is driven by other factors. For example, suppose an agency needs to contract a construction firm to build a storm drainage system. There are many companies across the country. But suppose there was only one in that city. All other firms would have to bring in workers and equipment from out of town, which would add greatly to the cost. So the one local firm may be the only one able to do the project for that price.

Sole Source contracts can be problematic for government agencies. There are usually several vendors who thought that they should have been considered. Many will complain. Sometimes they file a formal complaint. This generally leads to a letter explaining the reason. Sometimes they complain to an elected official. This generally leads to several angry phone calls and results in expending time and energy in order to justify something that was already justified. But worst of all, some complain to the press. This results in half-baked headlines filled with inaccurate allegations. This can cause a level of turmoil that almost brings an agency to a standstill. When reporters and aspiring politicians start swarming in search of a scandal like sharks smelling blood, it is difficult to get any work done. Consequently, agencies are careful when they sole source. Don't count on this as a normal method of selling.

RFP

The RFP, or Request For Proposal is the mother of all procurement tools. This is the big Kahuna. It is sometimes referred to as a Request for Quote (RFQ). Government agencies invest a great deal of time and much energy in the writing of a Request for Proposal. If the RFP is for a large procurement such as a complex computer system, a major construction project, or a long-term service agreement, this can be quite a document. I have responded to RFPs in excess of 350 pages long (the response I submitted filled two large 3-ring binders)! Creating an RFP like this is a major project in and of itself. The prospect will often commission a large team of people to do extensive research into every aspect of the project. This can take weeks or even months. This team will often begin this process and come to realize that they do not know enough about the available products and services in the market. When this is the case, they may issue a Request for Information (RFI). This is similar to an RFP but with a few differences. The main differences are that it is less detailed and does not lead to a contract. It is simply a means by which the task force collects information from leading vendors in the market. So do not confuse the RFI with the RFP. But back to the RFP. Sometimes the agency will engage a consulting firm to help them create the RFP. This is not an inexpensive process, but is sometimes necessary.

The RFP seems like it has a lot of silly rules and directions. Why should you spend so much time and energy? Why not just send your standard proposal in your standard format? Well, imagine this scenario. A government agency spends several weeks in planning sessions. They write and distribute an RFI. They receive all the RFI responses and compile the information. They put together an RFP task force to research the needs for the project. These people are pulled away from their regular duties for several weeks. Then the agency invests thousands of dollars with a consulting firm to assist in the RFP writing. So after several months spent and thousands of dollars expended producing a very detailed 250 page RFP, they sit down to review your response to discover that you did not even properly follow the directions on page 6. How impressed do you think they will be with you?

RFPs are usually very comprehensive documents. There are several sections that are common to most large RFPs (though not necessarily in this order).

- Introduction/Overview
- Legal Mumbo-Jumbo
- Directions
- Background/Current Status

- Requirements
- Cost Information

Lets take a look at some of these sections. Please keep in mind that these sections may vary and specific information may appear in a section other than the one I place it.

INTRODUCTION/OVERVIEW: This will usually cover basic information such as the name of the entity, the name of the RFP (e.g. RFP # 10928 - North Creek Wastewater Plant Extension), history of the agency, current stats of the agency (number of employees, etc.), and mission statement. This is important. Not so much because it will tell you that much about the agency, but it will let you know what they think is important about their agency.

LEGAL MUMBO-JUMBO: Yes, you have to read this too. And no, you will not see the title "legal mumbo-jumbo". This may or may not be an actual separate section. But it will appear somewhere. You may find that much of this does not apply to you. Many agencies require a common set of legal statements be included in any RFP that goes out the door. The same language is included whether the RFP is for a sophisticated laser surgical device, a dump truck, or manure to fertilize the county golf course. You may be proposing some type of consulting service that is billable at $250 per hour. Do not be surprised if the RFP has language requiring that every employee you bring to the project be paid at least minimum wage (I have seen this one before). Remember, this language covers all RFPs. This is obviously a concern with some types of contracted services. I was once reading an RFP from a State that had several environmental initiatives. Even though the RFP was for a sophisticated computer software system, there was a section describing the State's preference to purchase products made of recycled material (I actually had a couple of competitors who would have fit this bill quite well)! But read on nonetheless. Occasionally you will find something that does pertain to your company. It may be a requirement involving ownership of your company, State of incorporation, or the nation of incorporation of your insurance company.

One of my government jobs involved the review of financial documents of contractors wanting to do business with us. One of our requirements was that the firm must carry a certain minimum level of insurance from a sound insurance company. I was reviewing the financials of a firm (call them ABC). ABC owned a controlling share (90%) of a holding company in the Caribbean. This holding company was the sole owner of a small insurance firm also in the Islands. And guess who this small insurance firm's biggest client was? You guessed it, ABC Company! What's more, the reserve requirement rules in this particular country are quite a bit different than here and the majority of the insurance firm's assets were in ABC stock! So if the ABC went under and could not finish the project, what insurance coverage would they really have? None. The taxpayers would end up footing the bill. When you come across government procurement rules that seem pointless, be patient. Believe me, there really are reasons most of these rules were put in place!

DIRECTIONS: RFPs have directions. Follow them! End of story! If the directions state that your price information should be on a separate sheet in a sealed envelope with a specific set of information printed on the envelope, just do it the way they ask! RFPs list the names and contact information for the points of contact. Use them! Do not try to circumvent the contacts listed in the RFP (hopefully you can build relationships with people in the account before the RFP hits the street).

This section will often include the timetable information. Often there are specific time frames with deadlines to request extensions, ask questions, prepare your response, and submit your response. If the deadline for submittal is 11:00 AM on the 25th, don't be upset if you are ejected from the bid if your proposal comes in on the 26th. Do not be surprised if this happens when your proposal comes in on the 25th but at 2:00 PM. In fact, do not be surprised if you run in the door with your proposal at 11:01 AM and you get disqualified! Most government agencies are serious about these deadlines. Again, it may seem silly. But imagine this scenario, you come in five minutes late, and the agency makes an exception and accepts your proposal anyway. Then two days later, XYZ company brings their proposal in and is rejected. Two weeks later (just as you are signing your contract), XYZ company's lawyers are at the state capital filing a grievance as well as a civil rights suite. It does not matter that you were only five minutes late and XYZ was 48 hours late. The rules were clear. An exception was made for you, and not for XYZ. Now the government agency's project is on hold. The people involved with the project are now filling out paperwork and giving statements to the agency's legal staff. It is a big ugly mess. Again, there are very good reasons for most of these rules.

The directions will often include a list of the expected documents. These may include financial statements, insurance certificates, business license information, certificate of surety, bonding information, ownership declaration, etc. I have sat through bid openings and watched large detailed proposals from respected vendors tossed because they were missing one piece of required documentation. This is a similar situation to the one involving missed deadlines. The government agency simply cannot make exceptions.

This section will also usually give detailed information regarding the format of your proposal. It will often specify precisely how your proposal needs to be organized. This can be to a degree of detail that seems unbelievable. They may dictate how you will number your sections and subsections, how many words you can have in response to a certain requirement before you have to reference an attachment, what types of documents you are allowed to attach, and even down to the font and point size of your text. You may be required to submit it electronically as a TXT file, PDF, Word Doc, or other format. You may be required to submit your proposal in hard copy only. You also may be required to submit a large number of copies. So do not be surprised to see something like this in the requirements:

All text response shall be submitted in hard copy. Vendor shall utilize standard 8.5" by 11" white, non-glossy stock (the county prefers the use of recycled paper although it is not a requirement). The print shall be in black ink only. The typeface shall be in Times New Roman font with a point size of 12. There shall be no italics nor bold type used. Single underlining is permissible. The proposal shall be printed on the front and back of each sheet of paper so as to minimize the amount of paper being used. The proposal shall not be bound. Each page shall either be of the 3-hole type stock or of standard stock that has been punched by a 3-hole punch. Pages of the proposal shall be contained with a standard 3–ring binder. The binder shall be plain white or black in color. It should be the type with a clear vinyl slot in the front to hold a title page. You shall include a title page on plain white stock with black text only. The title page shall include the RFP number, the name of your company, and the name of your contact person with phone number and email address. The font for the RFP number and the name of your company may be up to a size of 14 points (but still must be Times New Roman). The contact person's name and number shall be in 12 point only. The RFP number shall be listed first, followed by your company's name. Both should be centered on the page. The contact information should appear in the lower right hand corner of the page………………

Not all RFP directions are this bad, but they do exist. When you see these types of instructions, don't think about it too much. Just grab a cup of coffee and go to it.

BACKGROUND: Okay, this is where the good stuff starts! This is the section that starts giving you some good information with regard to planning your strategy. This often discusses how things are done now, the reason the agency needs to change what they are doing, and sometimes the process leading up to this point. This will be very different based on the agency and the product or service needed. Suppose the RFP is for the construction of a new rail extension and station. This section will discuss the current rail system. It may talk about the extensive population growth in a particular suburb in the last ten years. It will discuss the increasing traffic on the roadways. It may talk about the urban traffic task force and the report they made recommending the rail extension. It then may discuss some of the obstacles to overcome. You get the idea.

REQUIREMENTS: This is the real substance of the RFP. This is the piece that takes so long to put together. This is the section that has the detailed functional requirements and deliverables expectations. This is where the agency tells you exactly what it is they want. A lot of due diligence usually goes into this. The legal requirements, deadlines, submission formats, and such usually originate with the purchasing department. But the requirements section originates with the real buyers. This was put together by the people who are actually driving the procurement. In other words, this was put together by the actual buyers. These sections are very different based on the type of procurement. Sometimes, they include a list of deliverables. Sometimes it will contain a functional table with checkboxes and room for comments. There are sometimes essay-type questions asking you to describe how your service will accomplish what the agency wants accomplished with this project. The key here is to make sure you respond to all of it and do not fabricate anything! After you win the contract, this document may be referenced. Make sure that you can backup anything you state in the proposal. If you say that your company can do it, you had better be able to do it.

COSTS: You will need to provide a price table, cost schedule, cost proposal, or some type of estimate. Be very clear about what you are doing here. The cost proposal you provide in response to the RFP cannot be a quickie estimate. If there are unknown variables, discuss them in detail. If a certain number is an estimate, state that it is an estimate and explain your assumptions. Be very detailed. You will have a chance to discuss all of this later, but make sure you do not put something in the proposal that is unclear or inaccurate. Depending on the rules of the procurement, the proposal you provide as a response to the RFP may be attached to the contract and you may be held liable for every word of it.

In summary, you do need to make sure your company can effectively respond to RFPs as well as meet the procedural requirements. The RFP alone will frighten some of your competitors away. Government RFPs are not for wimps. Only the strong will survive!

CHAPTER VII

What Do I Do Next?

I was very excited. It was my first week with a new company. I had interviewed long and hard in very stiff competition for this position. It was a dream job. The company had a product that was already selling very successfully in the private sector. It was just then beginning to get traction in the public sector, so my timing seemed to be just right. My position was newly created and would focus exclusively on the public sector. Every public sector account within my geographic territory was mine. I would make my own territory plan and run it like my own business. The sales director who hired me had created this position and was a firm believer in the potential rewards of a vibrant public sector practice. He was going to give me a long ramp-up time to get the public sector sales cycles going. The new company was doing everything I had always said should be done everywhere else I had worked. It was the open book I had always wanted. I had a week to put a preliminary territory plan together. My confidence was extremely high and there was not a question in my mind that I would deliver an excellent presentation listing the accounts in my territory, their budgets, number of employees, as well as my list of "top 40" accounts along with my marketing plan for those accounts.

I started doing the research. The territory covered two states along with the numerous state agencies. But there were also approximately 10 cities of sufficient size to be viable prospects for our product. There were also about 30 counties large enough. About 35 universities and 42 hospitals fit the bill also. A little more digging uncovered 10 public power utilities, 36 public water departments, 23 sewer districts, 4 port authorities, 3 bridge authorities, 6 transit authorities, and about 20 or so other assorted government and quasi-government accounts! Just like selecting that essay topic in school, I realized that I needed to narrow my scope and focus on one segment.

Market Focus

Obviously you will need to focus your efforts on some logical subset of the large group of state and local government entities. Some of this may be facilitated by virtue of the product or service you sell. For example, suppose that your company sells mobile phones and mobile phone service. Your territory includes dozens of state agencies who would normally be very good prospective customers. But you find out that the state government just signed a statewide agreement with a national firm to standardize all state agencies on this firm's equipment and services. Well, those dozens of state agencies have just been disqualified for you! Perhaps it is time to focus on the counties and cities. Some products and services may be provided internally by the government entity. You may represent a firm that contracts out custodial services to office buildings, but the city may actually have their own job positions for Custodian I, Custodian II, etc. Now that does not mean they will never change their minds and decide to outsource someday if you can prove a great ROI for them, but it may make more sense to go where these services are already outsourced and the contract is up at the end of the year. You may also encounter various legal or policy issues that will automatically disqualify many prospects for you. Perhaps your company is incorporated in another state or is foreign owned. Most governments prefer to buy locally when possible and some have requirements about domestic ownership. So once you eliminate the prospects that look like they are absolute non-starters, what do you do next?

While the following method of organizing your approach may be different for different industries and geographies, it can serve as a good starting point. Even if you choose not to use this method, you must use some method to avoid wasted time and resources.

Account Prioritizing

1 Existing Customers: If your company has a base of government customers who are already using your product or service, they are priority one. This is not related specifically to government, but to selling in general. We all have heard that it is much easier to keep a customer than to get a customer. If have an existing contract with a government agency, do not lose it to a competitor!

2 Existing Relationships: This is also nothing specific to government sales. If you have former business or personal connections to decision makers (or influencers) in government agencies, use them! Some salespeople (particularly new ones) are sometimes reluctant to do this. You should not be. There is nothing wrong with it. It is totally ethical to speak with people you know and

ask them if they are aware of any needs you can help to fulfill. It is okay to ask them to introduce you to someone else who may help. There is nothing at all wrong with this as long as favors or money do not change hands. This reluctance often comes from new salespeople who have been hired from government agencies based on their technical knowledge in some area of government. It would not be an uncommon occurrence for someone to leave a position at a government health department to work for a company selling medical testing equipment to government health departments. Who knows the business better? It makes sense for all parties, as this new salesperson will be able to match the best products to the right customers very quickly. But these new salespeople are sometimes reluctant to contact people they know for appointments. Don't be. Take your old friends out to lunch once a month on your company's dime and stay in the loop. Continue your professional memberships and stay active in conferences. Your old contacts will be happy to let you know when they hear about a sales cycle starting up somewhere.

3 References: Your company's products and services may have had great success in the past in specific areas. For example, your company may have almost no large cities as customers. They also may have few small towns as customers. But suppose your company has a very large number of happy customers who are municipalities with a population between 75,000 and 100,000? Then of course it makes perfect sense to start calling into other accounts in that size range. If you have a good set of success stories and happy customers to point to, this is the way to go. There is also a strong possibility within a reasonable geographic area that a public works manager in one city this size will know the public works manager in neighboring cities. They often attend the same seminars and conferences. It is also quite common for people to move from one

government entity to another. Someone who does an out standing job as the Assistant City Attorney in Southville may be offered the number one position in Northville.

4 Target Entity: This approach is very similar to what you may do if you have a strong reference base. You essentially try to determine what particular entities you may have the most success with and target those. Your target may be something similar to the following: K-12s with a student population greater than 5,000, counties with a population less than 200,000, all port authorities, all sewer districts, etc. You may determine these targets based on a number of criteria. The criteria may be the applicability of your particular product or service. It may also be a market trend or government regulation that creates a need for your product or service. But by focusing, you can tailor you presentations and become more knowledgeable regarding your prospect's needs.

5 Target Operation: Picture a grid on a sheet of paper or your computer, much like a spreadsheet. Imagine that across the top row are the names of various entities such as City of Penrose, Washington County, North County Port Authority, etc. Under each entity (city, county, etc.) would be a list of the various departments such as Finance, HR, Facilities, Administration, Motor Pool, and so on. The functional specialty approach involves identifying a particular department or function that exists in a variety of government entities. Motor Pools are a good example. Many government agencies have fleets of vehicles that are used by employees for business. Employees reserve these vehicles and sign them out much in the same fashion as you would reserve a car from a commercial car rental agency. If your company sells heavy duty cleaning supplies that happen to work extremely well on grease, you could target the motor pools of various agencies. You can often find information on these operations in newsletters or

professional organizations (like the National Association of Fleet Administrators).

This is by no means the only method of organizing and focusing your efforts, but it is at least a start.

Pursuing The Market

Assuming you have done your research and now have a target list of agencies you want to contact, what now? If you used the previous method of organizing your accounts, those falling into the first two categories are pretty simple. If you have an existing customer you simple call in and offer to meet with them to make sure everything is going well, etc. If you already have a relationship with someone, you simply invite him or her to lunch to discuss your new job and to catch up on things. The last three categories are another story. These are people who often have never heard of you or your company. This is back to the old standard sales routine of prospecting. As we all know, this is the tough part.

You have to make contact with a stranger and convince them that they should meet with you. It is not easy. In fact, it is hard. It is very hard. It involves putting yourself on the line. It involves the risk of embarrassment, and rejection. It involves uncertainty and requires unfaltering courage, confidence, and self- discipline. This is why very few people have what it takes to be successful sales professionals. This is also why sales professionals often earn the pay we do. So back to the topic, how do we prospect here? Lets look at the some of the most common prospecting methods.

Cold Calling

For the most part, this is tough in the public sector. It can work depending on your product or service. If you sell a low-dollar commodity and the buyer has no brand allegiance, then this can work, "just try 100 boxes at half price to see how you like them". But you generally will never get to high level decision makers via a cold call. And yes, I have read the books and been to the classes that tell you to call at 6:00 AM or 8:00 PM when the C-level person is in his/her office and the gatekeeper is not there. The gatekeeper is not there, but neither is the director you want to talk to. And if the director is there, he/she has something pretty pressing to deal with and your chances of getting a warm welcome are pretty slim. I won't say it can never work. I am sure someone has a great sales story about calling a director at 10:00 PM with the solution to the very problem that has that director working late. But don't build a marketing strategy around it. You can burn a lot of time cold calling trying to get to public officials. Your time would be better spent in the parking lot pounding your head against the pavement. Well, maybe that is an exaggeration, but you get my drift. Please do not totally discount cold calling as a valuable selling tool in the government space. Just do not think you can use it to get an appointment with VITO (for those of you new to sales, ask some of the experienced reps around you who VITO is, they will be happy to explain).

Cold calling can be very useful to get access to lower level people in the organization just to get in the door and find out what is going on there. These people can be very enthusiastic and can provide you with a lot of great information. Please, don't let yourself be fooled into thinking they can help push a deal through for you (even if this person believes they can do so). So cold calling for information gathering appointments can be very useful. Just be aware of what it can and cannot do for you.

Direct Mailing and Emailing

This approach in the public sector has almost the exact same effect it has in the private sector. Again, if you are new to sales, ask the experienced reps what they think. If your company has had great success with mailers in the private sector, then you should have some degree of success in the public sector also. If they have been a failure for your company and product in the private sector, expect similar results.

Networking

If you sell any high dollar products or services, networking is the best way to contact your prospects. Networking allows you build brand awareness not just for your company, but also for you personally. This works in a similar fashion to the private sector, with one major difference relating to networking outside an organization.

Imagine the following scenario. Your company sells consulting services that help computer software companies overcome their major software development problems. These are the problems and bugs that seem to keep coming back causing continual difficulties for software designers. You decide to host a round table discussion as a marketing event. You invite the top software designers from the five largest software companies (who shall remain nameless) to come to the event and discuss their biggest software bugs and problems in a supportive and sharing atmosphere in order that everyone there can help to find some mutually beneficial solutions to the others' problems. Okay, back to reality. First of all, some of these guys hate each other with a passion. None of them would come. If they did, you would have to frisk them at the door. They compete viciously for the same slices of pie in the marketplace. Anything that helps out "the other guy" has a direct negative impact on their income, retirement, and stock options. Secondly, they do not like to admit they even have software bugs (I once worked for a software company that did not allow the use of the word "bugs" but instead referred to them as "undocumented features"). And they certainly would not want to discuss their internal problems with the opposition! Almost every tiny bit of information these companies have is confidential and proprietary. They do not want to share anything. You would have this event and no one would say anything. They would all be there hoping the other guy would slip and let out some good competitive information. The situation is very different in the public sector.

If you were to present a similar event for government professionals, the outcome would be very different. Suppose you were to host a round table discussion on recruiting and retaining healthcare professionals in government. You would invite representatives from the HR departments of every large city, county, and state health department in your geography. If they were available, you would probably have a good turnout. You would most likely have a very open, sharing, and articulate group. They would probably be very up front in discussing their successes as well as their failures. They would be very happy to share ideas for improvements with each other. There is no threat. They would not worry that the neighboring county health department will try to steal business by persuading impoverished families to come to their county for government funded vaccinations. Your attendees would be public servants. Most of them really do believe in service. Most government professionals want to serve the public and help people. If they can share professional ideas or techniques that assist a fellow public servant in another locale, they are usually delighted to do so!

What does all this mean to you as a sales professional? It means that the Chief of Police in the city that already owns your product probably knows the Chief of Police in the neighboring city where you are trying to sell your product. It also means that this Chief of Police has no reason not to tell the other guy everything he knows about you, your product, your company, and the success or failure they have had with your product. He will also have no problem discussing exactly how much he paid. This is generally a matter of public record anyway. Don't give someone a "sweet deal" unless you want everyone else to ask for the same deal! How do these police chiefs know each other? Maybe one of them was the assistant police chief for the other before his/her current position opened up. They probably also are both involved in the Police Chiefs Association, the Association of Municipalities, the Policeman's Benevolent Association, or a dozen other groups. Networking and word of mouth can go a long way in the public sector.

Membership Organizations

Virtually every profession in government has at least one professional member organization. A quick web search with some key words will yield an unbelievable number of organizations. Go to any of the major search engines and type in the words

Government, Association, and then whatever profession you are interested in (accounting, food service, fleet management, etc.). These organizations often have corporate sponsor or associate membership available to allow some participation by vendors. These groups know you are there to network and build relationships in order to sell. But they do not mind. They need to buy products and services and they generally appreciate you taking the time to really understand their issues. Participation in these groups is one of the best ways to develop relationships as well as educate yourself in the world of your customer. You will learn a lot and have the opportunity to meet some very interesting people (maybe even some archeologists)!

SUMMARY

Well, there you have it. I truly hope this little book has been helpful to you. The intention was to give you some insight into the world of selling to state and local government. If you know more now than when you started to read it, then it was a success. If you were considering a career selling to state and local government and after reading this book have decided it is not for you, then it was also a success. If this is the case, you may have saved yourself a lot of unnecessary stress and anguish. But if this book has excited you about the prospect of selling to state and local government, great! Welcome to a very exciting and potentially lucrative career.

Thank you and best of luck. Happy selling!

- Charlie

HELPFUL WEBSITES TO GET STARTED

Governing Magazine - http://governing.com/

National Association of State Procurement Officials - http://www.naspo.org/

National Institute of Governmental Purchasing - http://www.nigp.org/

Government Procurement Journal - http://www.govpro.com/

National Governor's Association - http://www.nga.org/

National Conference of State Legislators - http://www.ncsl.org/

National League of Cities - http://www.nlc.org/

Institute of Supply Management - http://www.napm.org/

International City/County Managers Association - http://www.icma.org

U.S. Conference of Mayors - http://www.usmayors.org/

National Association of Counties - http://www.naco.org/

EPA Environmentally Friendly Purchasing - http://www.epa.gov/oppt/epp/

ABOUT THE AUTHOR

After high school, Charlie worked in various sales positions in his native Southern California. Following a stint in the military he relocated to the Midwest and began selling office equipment while completing his BA degree in Accounting. Charlie then worked in a variety of information technology, accounting, and auditing positions in the public sector. After completing a Masters in Business Administration several years later, he moved to the private sector selling computer software to state and local government.

Charlie still works in the software industry and lives with his family in New Jersey. He can be contacted via email at tbonecharlie58@netscape.net

Printed in the United States
27924LVS00001B/346

9 781418 460723